HOW TO FIGHT

YOUR

TRAFFIC TICKET

&

WIN !!!

206 TIPS, TRICKS & TECHNIQUES

D1739014

========================

MEL LEIDING, ATTORNEY AT LAW

===

AVENIR INTERNATIONAL PUBLISHING

1210 N. Jefferson St., STE. G, Anaheim, CA 92807
(714) 630-0141   Fax: (714) 666-8663

For permission write, fax or call:

Avenir International Publishing,
1210 N. Jefferson St., Ste. G, Anaheim, CA 92807
(714) 630-0141   Fax: (714) 666-8663

Library of Congress Catalog Card Number:
97-77718

ISBN: 1-891693-11-5

Printed in the United States of America

DISCLAIMER

TABLE OF CONTENTS

SUMMARY OF TOP TEN TIPS

Summaries are supposed to be at the end of a chapter or book not at the beginning. However, in this case I want to give you this summary of the top ten tips in the beginning so you can be thinking about them as you read each tip. I want you to see the forest before you see the trees. By the way tips 1-3-5 & 10 are the top of the top ten. Each of the top ten will be elaborated on in the following sections.

001. Have the **right attitude** towards the officer at the time of the stop. A rude or antagonistic type attitude will insure that you get a ticket and fix you solidly in his memory.

002. Always say you're sorry and **ask for a warning**. If you don't ask you won't receive. See tip number 79 for the best way to ask.

003. Always, without fail **plead Not guilty.** This gives you every advantage without any disadvantages. You can change your mind later without consequences. Just plead by certified mail. See tip number 138.

004. **Proper preparation** for a hearing is important. Write down everything that occurred and that was said at the time of the stop. Return to the scene to take photos, measurements, make diagrams etc. See preparation section.

005. Your ticket will be **dismissed if** the police **officer can't show** at the hearing for any reason. You have won without saying a word in your defense. In many cities there is a 50% to 60% chance the officer won't show resulting in your ticket being dismissed and your money returned.

006. In the courtroom you must have a proper and respectful **attitude toward the judge**, the officer and the court. If you don't you'll lose.

007. **Don't argue** with the officer or his testimony **when asking him questions in court.** Just ask your prepared questions and wait for the answer. If he was wrong or mistaken you can explain this to the judge after you've finished your questions.

008. Give a **detailed and truthful story** of what really happened from beginning to end. This is much more believable than a short simple statement that you didn't do it and the officer is wrong.

009. In your statement to the judge include and emphasize any **unproven elements** of your offense and explain any **valid defenses** you may have. See the following appropriate sections.

010. Always end by asking the judge to take your case **under submission**, meaning to delay his decision until he has done something like look at the scene or anything else outside the courtroom.

I. HOW TO AVOID GETTING FUTURE TICKETS

011. Try to be inconspicuous, invisible and unnoticeable to the police by not drawing attention to yourself in the way you drive.

012. Don't weave in and out of traffic or make excessive lane changes to move ahead of the traffic in front of you. If a police officer sees this he will start to watch you. You become a prime target for a ticket.

013. Don't tailgate to try to get the car in front of you to move out of your way so you can go faster. This invites a speeding ticket.

014. Try to stay out of the fast lane. Officers expect fast lane drivers to speed and watch them more closely than middle or slow lane drivers. Especially don't tailgate with your lights on in the fast lane to get cars to move out of your way.

015. Get slower cars ahead to move out of your way by flashing your high beams at them, day or night, from a safe distance and without tailgating.

016. Don't be the leader of the pack. If you are ahead of and pulling away from a pack of cars, this will bring you to the attention of the officer.

017. You can explain, if true, that you weren't the leader of the pack but the follower of the pack in front of you or maybe the pack you were "leading" was going below the speed limit because they saw the police car.

018. Follow a **scout car**. Stay safely behind a speeding car that passes you. That car acts as your scout and scouts ahead for radar and the police. The scout car will get stopped - not you. Don't follow too closely so the officer can't stop both cars.

019. Make a habit of constantly scanning for police vehicles by looking in your side and rear view mirrors and checking the blind spots by your right and left rear fenders. Your blind spot is often used by officers to pace your car for speed.

020. At night constantly pay attention to traffic behind you. Watch for unknown headlights or fast approaching vehicles which may be police. You will also be aware of unsafe tailgaters, drunk and other erratic drivers.

021. Watch the traffic far ahead of you. If you see brake lights come on, they probably saw a cop or an accident. Slow down and pay attention.

022. Watch oncoming traffic that may be signaling you that there is Radar ahead by flashing their lights or waving and pointing.

023. Equip your car with a CB radio and a good Radar Detector, if legal. They will tell you where the police and radar are waiting. It's better to hide the detector so the officer won't see it and it won't get stolen.

024. Always drive with your seat belt on. A marginal speeding ticket may be overlooked but marginal speed plus no seat belt will be ticketed.

025. The type of car you drive does draw attention. Corvettes, Ferraris, bright colored sports cars in the fast lane are watched more closely than generic four door family cars in the middle or slow lanes. Sports cars are expected to speed.

026. Drive a clean car both inside and out. This includes eliminating bumper stickers, window decals, etc. No matter what they say they have the potential to insult someone. A grade school emblem may upset an officer if his child was just kicked out of that school.

027. There is one exception to the no sticker rule. A sticker indicating any emergency medical profession, such as ambulance, nurse, doctor or fireman, may be on the back of your car. Warning, never falsely impersonate any of these people.

028. Inspect your car for mechanical defects. Check the headlights, taillights, brake lights side mirrors, current registration tags and bald tires. These defects draw police attention to you.

029. Many times an officer won't stop a car going only 5 - 10 MPH over the limit but will stop the same car if it has a mechanical defect like a tail light out or bald, unsafe tires.

030. Carefully obey all laws when driving near schools, children, hospitals, senior citizen centers etc. Also use extra caution near dangerous road conditions like sharp curves, steep hills or road construction. These places are usually heavily patrolled which increases your chances of a ticket.

031. Traffic police have favorite spots where they know they can write many tickets. They go back to the same spots again and again to write tickets. Watch for and be careful at those spots.

032. Favorite hiding places to catch people are at the bottom of hills, just around curves, behind high fences, buildings, bushes and parked trucks. Another favorite place is cruising in front of a large camper or truck in the slow lane, waiting for a speeder to pass.

2. HOW TO HANDLE THE TRAFFIC STOP AND OFFICERS APPROACH

033. From the instant you realize you are being stopped you should begin setting a cooperative tone which will ease the officer's anxiety and put him in the right frame of mind to issue a warning instead of a ticket.

034. Traffic stops aren't routine. Hundreds of officers are injured or killed each year during these stops. They never know who is hostile and must view each stop as potentially dangerous and deadly. They are sensitive to even the slightest suspicious or antagonistic behavior or attitude.

035. Officers are people who have normal human emotions and reactions. If you insult or antagonize them they can become angry and will be sure to write up every possible violation against you.

036. A good attitude upon initial contact and the following proper procedures for pulling over will set the proper stage for a warning and hopefully no ticket.

037. Don't make the officer chase you. Pull over safely as soon as you know he wants you to. Remember Rodney King made them chase him.

038. If you quickly pull over and stop, this is an indication you are alert and paying attention to your driving. Use your emergency flashing lights.

039. Always pull over to the right side of the road. Never stop in the center median or mall.

040. Pull over far enough off the road so the officer can walk up and stand beside your car without worrying about being hit by passing traffic.

041. Once stopped, stay in your car and let the officer come to your window. People who exit their cars are more likely to attack or run.

042. Get prepared by slowly getting your registration and wallet or purse in plain view on the seat beside you. Don't take your license out until asked to do so by the officer.

043. If you must reach into your glove box or console while the officer is there, explain your actions and move slowly. Otherwise he doesn't know if you are reaching for a weapon.

044. Keep all other passengers in control, quiet and calm. They must keep their hands visible at all times and only speak if asked a question.

045. Roll down the drivers side front and rear windows and if it's night, turn on the interior lights so he can see there's nothing to fear inside.

046. Never throw anything out of the car when the officer is behind you. They always see it and become suspicious. It could add littering fines.

047. Remove your sunglasses. Don't make any sudden or surreptitious gestures or moves that could make him think you are hiding something under the seat like drugs, weapons, alcohol etc.

048. Keep your seat belts on so there is no question whether you were wearing it. Also the hand movement to undo your seat belt could be misinterpreted as reaching for a weapon or hiding something. Make sure all passengers remain properly seat belted.

049. Put both your hands on top of the steering wheel so he can see you have no weapons.

050. Take several deep breathes and try to stay calm. Getting upset at yourself or the officer will not help. The worst that will happen is you may get a ticket that you can fight and possibly win. On the other hand you might just get a warning.

051. It seems like forever but the average traffic stop is about 10 minutes plus time to check if the car is stolen. Be patient.

3. WHAT TO SAY TO THE OFFICER

052. Start off on the right foot with a nice, cooperative and respectful attitude. Say you're **sorry** and you hope he is having a better day than you. This sets up your forthcoming sob story or excuse. Don't say "Sorry I was going a little fast." because this can be interpreted as an admission.

053 . **ATTITUDE:** The most important thing you should learn from this book is to have a good attitude toward the officer and the situation. Most people talk their way into a ticket by being rude, antagonistic and disagreeable. Stay calm and don't argue.

054. Try to be inconspicuous and as unrememberable as possible so the officer won't recall much about you or giving you the ticket when he is in the courtroom months later.

055. If you are a jerk with a nasty attitude the officer will give you a ticket even if he originally had intended on giving you a warning. Also he will make copious detailed notes, including everything you say, to use against you in court.

056. Be honest and sincere with the officer. He does this every day and he will know immediately when you are being less than truthful.

057. There are thousands of pages of traffic laws and so many people driving that the officer knows he can write as many tickets as he wants. If he stops one person who is nice and friendly and another who calls him a jerk - who do you think will get the ticket. Watch your attitude.

058. Try to put yourself in the officers shoes doing his job and someone just insulted you or called you a liar. Would you give him a warning or a ticket?

058. Remember the way you say something is almost as important as what you say. If you say the right things but in an angry, rude or condescending manner - you can expect a ticket.

059. When you are stopped don't take it personally. This will only make you angry and result in a negative attitude. They are not after you specifically or personally. The officer doesn't have a list of names he is going to try to ticket that day.

060. A good attitude may result in a ticket for a reduced speed rather than your actual (higher) speed. This may reduce the amount of your fine.

061. Negative attitudes like anger, contempt, irritation, annoyance, harassment or indignation and being rude, discourteous, cranky, offensive or insulting will provoke an unnecessary ticket. These attitudes talk your way into a ticket.

062. A proper attitude may eliminate one or more lessor counts in a multi-violation situation. If you were speeding, ran a light, turned from the wrong lane without signaling and your taillight is out, he may overlook everything but the speeding. A nasty attitude will assure a ticket for all violations.

063. Try to present an attitude that tells the officer that you're just an ordinary person, not a criminal. Tell him you try to obey all traffic laws, that you will try harder in the future and you would appreciate just a warning this time.

064. If the officer has a bad attitude and is arrogant, insulting or rude to you don't let him get to you. Resist being sucked into his bad attitude. Try to remain calm and inconspicuous so he won't remember you .

065. If an officer is unnecessarily insulting to you, write down or tape record immediately after the incident, everything you remember that was said and how it was said so you won't forget any details.

066. When the officer's behavior is extremely confrontational, condescending and sarcastic towards you, put up with it by realizing he won't be such a wise guy in front of the judge or when your formal written complaint goes on his permanent record.

067. On the street, at the time of the traffic stop, is not a smart time to argue, fight or insult the officer no matter how nasty he is or how innocent you are. He will win and you will get a ticket or worse. A written formal complaint may be the best answer.

068. If the officers attitude and behavior are completely out of line you can file a written complaint with his superiors, the city council, the mayor and his mother. It must be factual and truthful. This will be investigated and go on his permanent record.

069. Written complaints should only be filed for extreme behavior and you should wait until after your hearing date to increase the chances he might not show for the hearing.

070. If the officer is courteous and gives you a warning you should always write a letter of recommendation to the same people you would have complained with. You could ask the officer where to send a recommendation if you wrote one on his behalf.

071. When the officer comes to your open window let him start the conversation. Never start first with anything like "Whats the matter cop - I didn't do anything wrong. Why are you stopping me?" or "Why aren't you out catching real criminals?" This kind of start will get you a ticket.

072. If you are asked "tricky" questions like "Do you know why I stopped you?" be careful. If you say "yes, because I ran the light." its an admission of guilt. If you say "No, I don't know.", then you weren't paying attention. Be noncommittal and vague like "I'm really not exactly sure."

073. If asked "Do you know how fast you were going?" be careful not to admit to speeding or to not knowing your speed. Just say "I believe I was going the speed limit." meaning safe and reasonable for the conditions.

074. The above types of questions are only asked to get you to admit to something that can be used against you in court. Always give a noncommittal, non insulting answer that doesn't accidentally admit to something.

075. When he asks for your license and registration is the best time to give an excuse and ask for a warning. If you have a police volunteer card, PBA card or badge make sure he sees it. If true, tell him your son, friend or brother is "on the job". Be careful, he may call in to check the name.

076. Don't ask "why" questions like "Why did you stop me", "Why should I give you my license", "Why aren't you arresting real crooks" etc. These are all considered antagonistic and will get you a ticket.

077. Try making some small talk with the officer. Ask how his day is going or his opinion about some current police related event. Show some interest in him and his job.

078. Give a rational, honest and sincere explanation of factually what happened without admitting guilt in any way. Then ask, don't beg, for a warning. If you don't ask you won't receive.

079. The following is the best way to ask the officer for a warning - but put it in your own words - "I know you're probably right officer - but I'm usually a very safe driver and I'm trying very hard to keep my record clean. Will you excuse me this time and just give me a warning. I promise I will be more careful."

080. If true a sympathetic story may help like "I've been homeless and I'm starting my first new job today. I'm really nervous and would appreciate it if you could help me out with just a warning or my dog just died and I'm not myself today.

081. The best time to tell the officer about your "excuse" or "reasons" for what happened and to ask for a warning is when you are getting out your license and registration. This is the only time he is your captive audience. When he has your license he can go back to his vehicle to write the ticket and it's usually too late.

082. Never ask the officer to "hurry up" or say you are "late." He won't hurry and this insinuates you were speeding or ran the light because you were late. These comments will be in his notes to use at trial.

083. Don't bombard the officer with frantic almost hysterical chatter in an attempt to dissuade a ticket. This will produce the opposite effect and possibly a ticket. It's better to stay calm and rational.

084. Crying as a tactic to get out of a ticket usually won't work. However, if you can't control yourself then let it all out. It may or may not help.

085. Never try to bribe an officer. This could result in more serious additional charges of attempted bribery.

086. Always remove your license from your wallet or purse so the officer won't have to worry about being accused of taking something and there is no chance of a mistaken bribery attempt.

087. Never accuse or insinuate that the officer stopped you because he is prejudice against you because you drive a sports car, an old car, a new car, you're a teenager, a senior citizen, have long hair or short hair or you belong to x, y or z race. This type of accusation will insure a ticket by forcing him to prove he's not prejudice but writes tickets for everyone equally.

088. Never name drop in an attempt to get out of a ticket. Officers hear this all the time and it rarely works. The police chief may be your friend's best friend but the officer might hate the chief because he didn't promote him. You might get a ticket because you name dropped.

089. Excessive use of words like "Sir" won't help as it is usually thought of as blatant sucking up. Just call him officer as this is neutral and shouldn't offend anyone.

4. HOW TO DEAL WITH TRICKY COP QUESTIONS

090. Never admit that you did anything wrong. He will note it for later use in court against you. It's better to be stupid, vague or noncommittal when answering questions than to inadvertently admit guilt. "Officer, I was only going 40 not 50" is an admission if the speed limit is only 35 MPH.

091. The officer takes notes and anything you say can be used against you in court. Usually the less said the better for you.

092. You don't have to answer any of the officer's questions about the facts surrounding the supposed violation and what you did or didn't do. Be careful because a rude refusal is counter productive. It's better to give a vague answer.

093. Don't admit you don't know something like your speed or that there is a stop sign. It's better to say you are not 100% sure but you think so etc. Be vague rather than accidentally admitting guilt.

094. Don't whine, beg or plead with the officer. It's better to be rational and logical.

095. Be cautious using humor. Traffic stops are not funny to most officers.

"He says that due to my disregard for the Vehicular Velocity Statutes, he's being forced to issue me a Certificate of Non-compliancy."

5. EXCUSES
WHICH ONES WORK AND
WHICH ONES DON'T
SOME GOOD & SOME BAD

096. Never lie. The officer is lied to daily and will know when you are not being truthful.

097. Emergencies are good if valid, serious and believable. Rushing someone to the hospital for a serious reason is good. Your child bleeding in the back seat or your wife having a baby in the back seat are valid. A child's ear infection probably is not. Expect a police escort to the hospital and if you are lying expect a ticket.

098. Remember an experienced officer has heard every excuse under the sun day in and day out. Therefore, for your excuse to be effective it must be original, creative and truthful.

099. Most mistakes, ignorance of the law or forgetfulness generally are not good excuses. Excuses like "I forgot that stop sign was there" or "I thought the speed limit was 35 not 25" won't work. These are also inadvertent admissions.

100. My speedometer, cruise control or throttle is broken won't work unless you can prove it just happened. This may be a legitimate justification in court if you bring evidence like a mechanics statement or a repair bill.

101. Being sick is not a good enough excuse for violating the law. Although diarrhea might be. If you or someone in your car is sick you can expect a ticket or an escort to the hospital.

102. As stated the fact that you have to go to the bathroom may be a justification to speed if you are believed.

103. I was just going with the "flow" of traffic, does not work and is considered an admission that you were speeding. "Everyone else was going 80 and I was just trying to keep up with them." This admits you and everyone else was speeding. He can only stop one at a time.

104. Tailgating on the freeways or expressways is not excused by stating "if I don't follow closely other cars will cut in front of me ". This is true but is viewed as an admission.

105. Excuses followed by begging and pleading for mercy or to be let go generally don't work. An excuse is an attempt to justify guilty behavior so it must be good and used with dignity.

106. "I'm sorry." Saying you're sorry by itself is not enough to get off or get a warning. Everyone is sorry after they are caught.

107. I'm sorry but --- (good excuse) like " I'm sorry but I just started the first job I've had in a year and I can't miss this meeting." (Don't say you're late for a meeting.) It must be an important, honest, sincere and immediate serious situation.

108. If you were forced to do something to avoid a serious accident this is usually acceptable if believable and verifiable. Some wild, crazy, erratic, drunk driver was chasing you and you were trying to get away or out of his way.

109. The best and most believable excuses are usually the truth of whatever really happened which can't be made up. Lifes unexpected twists and turns. So tell the truth.

110. Rushing home because you left the sausage cooking on the stove and you're afraid it will burn the house down is good, but the officer might follow you home to help put out the kitchen fire.
111. Even though a good excuse might not be a complete defense, try to use it in court as a mitigating circumstance to minimize and reduce your fine or DMV points.

6. THE BEST THINGS TO SAY IF YOU ARE GETTING A TICKET

112. If you get a ticket don't worry. You haven't lost yet. There are many ways to win. The fight has just begun. They won this battle but you can win the war. You have many more chances to win at the arraignment, plea bargain, hearing and appeal stages.

113. After the officer starts writing the ticket you should be quiet. The less said the better because it's usually to late to talk your way out of it. Be calm and forgettable. The less they remember about you the better.

114. After it's written the only thing worth saying is something that will make the officer think you have no intention to fight the ticket. "Officer can I just mail this in because I don't have time to go to the clerk to pay it." Or " Do I have to wait for something in the mail or can I just go down and pay it now?"

7. SIGNING AND ACCEPTING THE TICKET

115. Always sign the ticket when asked and sign without any dissent. It is only a promise to appear and not an admission of guilt.

116. Refusal to sign the ticket puts your identity in question. This may result in your being taken into custody and brought to court for an arraignment before the next available judge. You could be in jail for several days if it is a long weekend. It's smarter to sign the ticket and stay out of jail.

117. Always sign your real name as it appears on your license. If you sign a false or fictitious name this is a separate misdemeanor.

118. Signing Mickey Mouse is not funny to the officer or the court. It puts your identity in question and gives them reason to hold you in jail.

119. If the officer asks you questions while you are signing be careful. He is trying to get you to inadvertently admit guilt. Give vague answers or answer his question with your own questions.

120. Accept the ticket with dignity and invisibility. Do not act indignant and snatch the ticket out of his hand. Just quietly accept it. Don't do anything that will make him remember you.

121. Do not make any wise guy remarks and above all don't say " I'll see you in court." These comments tip him off that he must make numerous notes and get prepared for court.

122. Don't argue, debate or disagree with him. You don't want to be remembered or let him know you are going to fight this ticket.

123. Never tear up your ticket in front of the officer and throw it out the window. The ticket has important information that may be needed in your defense. Information like wrong car, wrong date or wrong code section etc. Also you will probably get a second ticket for littering.

124. Always drive off in a normal speed and manner. If you spin your wheels and fishtail onto the street you invite another ticket and you have made yourself highly unforgettable.

125. Be polite, courteous and inconspicuous. Remember your day in court will come.

8. DECIDE TO FIGHT YOUR TICKET

126. You should decide to fight your ticket as soon as you get it or at least within the next few days so you can begin preparing while things are still fresh in your mind.

127. In America you are innocent until proven guilty beyond a reasonable doubt. Fighting your ticket simply means the officer (state) must prove it's case against you. There are plenty of chances for them to screw up. Make them prove it.

128. There are many reasons to fight your ticket. To save money on fines, to avoid insurance rate increases, save points on your license, to stand up for your rights, to feel better about yourself by not being pushed around by the bureaucracy, because the cop was a jerk or because you are innocent. All are good reasons to fight your ticket.

129. There is no reason not to fight your ticket. If you lose you are in no worse position than if you had plead guilty and paid the fine.

9. ALWAYS PLEAD NOT GUILTY

130. Always plead not guilty. A no contest or guilty with an explanation plea is just another way to plead guilty and insure you lose.

131. By pleading not guilty you automatically have about a 50 - 50 chance the officer can't show and you win without any effort on your part in court.

132. A not guilty plea gives you many options and opportunities to win that are eliminated along with your rights when you plead guilty.

133. If you plead not guilty and pay your ticket as bail and for any reason you can't go to the hearing there are no additional consequences. You forfeit the bail which is the same as if you had paid the ticket in the first place. So you might as well plead not guilty because you have nothing to lose.

10. THE ARRAIGNMENT

134. The arraignment is a means by which the court informs you of your rights and the charges against you. It is also the time when you hopefully plead **not** guilty and get a hearing date.

135. Your basic rights for traffic tickets are: 1. a trial within 45 days of the arraignment (your right to a speedy trial), 2. right to question witnesses for or against you and to subpoena witnesses or things for you., 3. to remain silent or to testify on your own behalf, 4. right to reasonable bail, 5. right to an attorney or to represent yourself, 6. a right to a court trial or a jury trial in about half the states.

136. Your pleading choices are: A . plead not guilty, pay the fine as bail and ask for a court date. Your bail is returned when you win, B. plead guilty, pay the fine and suffer all the points & insurance consequences, C. plead guilty with an explanation, which is really a guilty plea, D. plead nolo contendre, which is a guilty plea but it can't be used against you in a civil trial (accident cases).

137. There are three ways to have an arraignment. 1. Go to court before the judge. 2. Go to the traffic clerks window and plead not guilty, request a hearing date and pay the fine as bail. 3. Plead not guilty by certified mail, request a hearing and pay the fine as bail.

138. The best, fastest and easiest way is by certified mail to the address on the ticket back. Send a copy of the ticket with a letter waiving a formal arraignment. Say you are hereby pleading not guilty and requesting a court date. You are enclosing a check in the amount of the fine as bail. The court will send you a hearing date.

139. On your ticket above your signature and promise to appear is the date, time and place for arraignment. You must appear on or before that date either before the court, clerk or by mail.

140. Always send your not guilty plea by certified mail return receipt requested. This along with your cancelled check will prove you responded in time.

141. If your only objective is to reduce your fine then you should go to the arraignment. You can usually plea bargain and reduce the fine in exchange for a guilty plea.

142. You must pay your ticket (bail) at the time of the arraignment but it will be returned to you if your case is won or dismissed.

143. An arraignment continuance is normally granted one to three times by requesting it from the traffic court clerk or in court. This can give you more time to raise money for bail, to prepare a defense and for the officers memory to fade.

144. If you are nervous about the court arraignment find out when they are held and visit one time before your date.

145. At the arraignment don't be talked into a trial by written declaration. This means the officer doesn't have to show and you will almost always lose. It is better to plead not guilty.

146. If you decide to plead (not guilty) by going to the traffic court clerk window, try to go when there are no lines. Usually there are lines in the morning between 8:00 AM and 10:30 A.M. in large cities. Call the clerk and ask when is the best time to avoid the lines.

II. TRAFFIC SCHOOL

147. Most courts allow you to attend traffic school as an alternative to pleading guilty or going to court. You still must pay the fines and an additional fee and school costs. The offense will not count against your DMV record or be reported to your insurance. Therefore, no insurance rate increases or loss of points.

148. Traffic school is restricted to certain time periods which vary but are usually from 18 months to two years. It applies to only one violation within the period not one ticket with multiple violations. If it's one ticket for two offenses like speeding and a stop sign, only one is eligible.

149. Save points and insurance rates by attending traffic school. You can request it at the clerk's window, at the arraignment (required in some courts) and sometimes in court before your hearing begins. Some judges call all cases then give the traffic school option after you know if your officer showed up.

150. If you plead guilty or are found guilty and traffic school is part of your sentence this different and doesn't save points or insurance rates.

12. HOW TO PREPARE
FOR COURT

151. Preparation is the most important thing you can do to increase your chances of winning in court. If you don't prepare or look like you're prepared you'll probably lose. Prepare at least a diagram or photos to show the judge.

152. At the time of or immediately after your ticket write down in detail everything you remember starting just before the stop until after the officer or you leave. This should include all other traffic, pedestrians, road work, road conditions, weather, obstructions, lighting conditions, location and description of all traffic signs & signals, visibility (heavy fog etc.) obstruction to vision from the officers line of sight, witnesses etc. Write in detail what the officer said and what you said.

153. If possible try to figure out speeds, times and distances so you can ask the officer related questions. For example how long (time) and for what distance did you pace me. What was my speed during the pace. Then check the figures to see if he was right. The more details you have, the more

questions you can ask the officer. The more questions the officer is unable to answer accurately the weaker his credibility and case become.

154. If there were any witnesses have them write down what they saw and remember. Then sign and date it. If favorable to your case you may be able to use this in court if the witness is unavailable.

155. Judges are impressed if you come to court with something visual & relevant to show them like photos of the scene and/or a diagram. It shows you are serious and believe in your case. Use the photos and diagram to show you are right and the officer is wrong or mistaken. Include measurements and relevant details in the diagram.

156. Return to the scene and if safe take many photos both general and specific. Take photos of the general location, of signs, of the road, of double yellow lines, of holes in the road, of anything that might have obscured the officers vision, trees covering the stop sign etc. Anything that will help your case or help you explain your case.

157. If safe take measurements of relevant distances, road width, height of obstructions etc. Use the measurements in your diagram, to supplement the photos and as a basis for questions at the hearing.

158. Put more emphasis on the evidence that will favor you and less on the evidence that might convict you. Consider blowing up photos to 8 X 10 size if they help your case.

159. Go to the public or law library and look up in the vehicle code the section you allegedly violated. Break it down into each element that the officer must prove and make sure he proves it in court. For example speeding - no person / shall drive/ a vehicle/ upon a highway/ at a speed that is greater than reasonable etc.

160. If you can disprove any element of your offense then you win. Maybe you weren't driving, it was a private road not a public highway and best of all your speed was safe and reasonable. All offenses can be similarly dissected and handled.

161. Next be prepared with about a dozen or more relevant questions to ask the officer that tend to show his mistakes & that you are innocence. Write them down but always be ready to explore his answers with more questions if necessary.

162. Write out your side of what happened so you can explain it to the judge after you've finished questioning the officer. Use the notes you wrote down immediately after the ticket so you won't forget anything. End your story with a request that the judge find you not guilty or take your case "under submission" so he can look at the scene.

163. Be prepared for the officer to put up his own diagram on the board for his use. Bring a red marking pen and when he is finished cross out anything that isn't right or add anything left out. Then put your diagram up over his so yours is remembered and viewed last.

SPEED, TIMES & DISTANCE CHART

MPH times 1.47 = Feet Per Second (FPS)

EXAMPLE: If the yellow light is 2.5 seconds, the intersection is 48 feet wide, you were going 20 mph and you were 10 feet before the intersection when the light turned yellow. You were out of the intersection when the light turned red.

20 MPH X 1.47 = 29.4 FPS X 2.5 seconds = 73.5'
73.5 - (48+10) = 15.5 feet past the intersection when the light turned red.

5 MPH = 7.35 FPS	45 MPH = 66.15 FPS
10 MPH = 14.70 FPS	50 MPH = 73.50 FPS
15 MPH = 22.00 FPS	55 MPH = 80.85 FPS
20 MPH = 29.40 FPS	60 MPH = 88.20 FPS
25 MPH = 36.75 FPS	65 MPH = 95.55 FPS
30 MPH = 44.10 FPS	70 MPH = 102.90 FPS
35 MPH = 51.45 FPS	75 MPH = 110.25 FPS
40 MPH = 58.80 FPS	80 MPH = 117.60 FPS

13. ABOUT THE COURT HEARING

164. Try to visit a traffic court hearing prior to the date of your hearing to see how it works. This will eliminate most of your fears and nervousness. Traffic hearings are very informal and last only about five minutes. The judge is neutral and even the worst cop becomes docile in front of the judge.

165. Go to the traffic clerks window and ask for a continuance of your court date. Try to get several continuances for different reasons. Each continuance increases the chance the officer won't show and if he does his memory of details will be weaker with the passage of time.

166. Absolutely no bad attitudes are tolerated in court. A good attitude towards the cop in the street was important but it is many times more important in the court. If you show even the slightest ill will towards the judge, the cop or the court you will lose or worse be held in contempt.

167. Never say the officer was lying. Say he was mistaken or confused. Never say he was hiding

or lying in wait even though this is what they do. Don't make any accusations that show disrespect. Above all don't argue with the officer, witness and especially not with the judge. You'll lose. Instead rationally discuss and logically present your side of the case.

168. What to wear. Dress conservatively. A suit and tie is good but not necessary. A collared shirt, slacks and shoes is sufficient. For females a conservative dress or skirt and blouse is good. Don't wear shorts, t-shirts, tank tops, dirty jeans and sandals. No sunglasses and no gum in the court. Most important is to be neat and clean.

169. Don't walk between your table and the judges bench without permission. If you want to give photos, a diagram or statement to the judge give it to the bailiff who will give it to the judge.

170. Look the judge in the eyes when you talk to him. Always be honest and sincere. Be yourself and use common everyday language. Speak slowly and clearly so you're easily understood. Don't raise your voice in anger.

171. Courtroom procedures vary but in a nutshell basically are as follows. a. Judge arrives and the bailiff tells everyone to sit down and be quiet. b. The Judge tells what he is going to do and then calls the names of the officer and defendant in each case to see who is there. If you're not there you

are found guilty and bail is forfeited. If you are there but the officer is not your case is dismissed, you win and can go home. Bail is returned by mail. c. Bailiff swears everyone in as a group. d. When your case is called you and the officer go to the table. The officer gives his canned testimony. You then question him if you want. When you have no further questions you give your side of the story, your defense and ask the judge to take your case under submission or advisement to look at the scene. The judge may ask you questions then find you not guilty, guilty or decide later and notify you by mail. You exit quietly.

172. The officer's testimony is usually very brief, about one minute. The basic testimony is about the same for each type of case with the names, dates and places changed. He reads a canned formula type testimony. You can and should object to him reading from anything (his notes) that isn't introduced as evidence. He should be testifying from his memory. If he reads from anything you have a right to see it.

173. Make a check list of the elements of the offense. Concentrate and make sure he covers and proves each element. If he doesn't prove an element don't ask him about it because this is like proving it for him. Tell the judge as part of your story that he failed to prove an element of the offense and request a dismissal of your case.

14. WHAT TO ASK THE OFFICER

174. When the officer is finished you will be asked if you have any questions. Do not say yes and then not ask questions but begin to argue or contradict what the officer said. For instance "officer you couldn't see the color of the light from where you were parked." This isn't a question but should be used in your statement. Ask questions first. Then point out his mistakes in your statement.

175. Have your basic questions written out or at least an outline of the areas you want to cover but be flexible and ready to expand to new areas depending on the answers you get.

176. Always know the answer to the questions you ask. This eliminates surprises and answers that can hurt your case.

177. Try to show inconsistencies in the officer's testimony. Then in your statement you can say he didn't really remember or he's not sure of his testimony. For example: first he said "no other traffic around" then he remembered the white car when asked. Try to show he couldn't' see and observe what he thinks he saw.

178. You should only ask questions that will help your case. If the officer left out an element of your offense don't question him about it because you are then establishing that part of his case for him. The right time to mention this is in your statement when it's too late for him to correct it.

179. Make the officer answer only your question and don't let him volunteer additional harmful information that's not in response to your question. Stop these non-responsive answers by interrupting and saying "excuse me, but that is not what I asked you. Please answer only my question."

180. Your attitude when asking questions is of extreme importance. Be calm, courteous and polite. You will get better answers and stay on the good side of the judge. Rude and antagonistic "grilling" will unnecessarily upset the judge.

181. When you have finished with your questions say "Your Honor, I have no further questions at this time." Then be quiet and let the judge ask if you have anything you want to say.

15. HOW TO TELL YOUR SIDE OF THE STORY

182. The whole purpose of your giving a statement of your side of the story is to **raise a reasonable doubt** as to your guilt. Try to use these words at least once in your statement. For example " because the officer can't see in two places at once raises a <u>reasonable doubt</u> that he saw the light" etc.

183. You want to present yourself as an honest and innocent person so the judge will like you and find in your favor. The best way to do this is to be yourself and tell your story in your own words without being phony or antagonistic.

184. Be prepared and know what you are going to say. Practice in the mirror. Make an outline to organize your thoughts and to insure you won't forget anything. Try not to read word for word.

185. Don't be over dramatic. If you overdo it you are less believable.

186. Get to the point immediately and concentrate on important facts only. Don't ramble on about marginally important points.

187. How to decide what to include and

what to leave out of your statement. Ask yourself what does this relate to, what does it prove and most importantly - does it help my case.

188. It is probably best not to try to use humor in your story unless the judge initiates humor or seems to be receptive to it in his court.

189. If you have your own diagram, map or photos, you should put them on the bulletin board or give them to the bailiff to give to the judge before you start speaking.

190.   You have a right to remain silent if you don't want to testify. In traffic ticket cases I think you should tell your story.

191. Your statement should consist of the following sections:
a. Your detailed version of the facts and how it all happened from beginning to end.
b. Your comments on the officers testimony such as he failed to prove an element beyond a reasonable doubt, and any mistakes or inconsistencies in his version of what happened.
c. Defenses establishing a reasonable doubt.
d. Ask the judge to take your case under submission or advisement.

192. When you testify give a detailed, complete version of the facts of the incident in a logical sequence from beginning to end. A simple

"I didn't do it" isn't enough. The more factual details you give the more believable you will be.

193. Be realistic, honest and accurate without making unbelievable exaggerations.

194. Do not contradict yourself. Even minor contradictions may influence the judge. If you say you were going 39 MPH and later say 38 MPH the judge will believe you didn't know your speed.

195. Help the judge by giving him reasons to find in your favor like, I wasn't driving, no proof the radar or speedometer was accurately calibrated, the officer couldn't see the color of my stop light from where he was parked, the other car was speeding not me, or his testimony was wrong.

196. In addition to factual defenses consider the defense of necessity in that it was the only way to avoid an accident. Defense of self or others by trying to get away from a car jacker or worse. Coercion or duress may be applicable. Extreme emergencies requiring you to speed to the hospital are valid. Be certain your defenses are truthful.

197. Always end by stating (something) establishes a reasonable doubt and therefore you should be found not guilty but if the judge wants to be sure he should take the case under advisement to drive by the scene so he can see for himself.

198. After you finished your statement be

ready in case the judge asks you a question like "were you speeding" or did you stop at the stop sign" etc. Don't lie but don't admit guilt either.

199. Bring a list of your monthly income and expenses to use to try to get your fine reduced or make installment payments by showing low income.

200. Check the vehicle code for minimum & maximum fines and ask for the minimum. Object and appeal to paying more than the maximum unless prior violations were proven or you admitted a prior. Remain silent rather than admit priors.

201. If you lose - lose with dignity. Don't make any disparaging remarks regarding the judge, the court or the officer. Don't stomp out and slam the courtroom door. I have seen people brought back and held in contempt of court for similar behavior.

202. You have a right to appeal if you lose. If you win the appeal you usually only win the right to have a new trial. You have a second chance to be better prepared.

16. TRUCKERS

203. Because your livelihood depends on your driving license you should fight every ticket you get. You should at least consult with an experienced attorney and hire one if the ticket jeopardizes your job or driving privileges. Every tip in this book applies equally to all truckers.

204. When the officer approaches you should stay in your cab with the light on, the door open and your hands visible to show there is no threat. Ask if he wants you to stay in the cab or to climb down. If you climb down bring all your paper work (permits, log book etc.) with you and leave the cab door open.

205. Be cooperative. Let him look in your cab if he wants to. Offer your paper work to him before he asks for it. Small talk and a friendly attitude will help you get a warning.

206. Ask him to give you a warning or an equipment ticket rather than a moving violation. Try to blame the trucking company in some way to make an equipment ticket seem like the right thing to do.

APPENDIX A

QUESTIONS

The main purposes for asking the officer questions at the hearing are to 1. disprove some part of his case 2. prove some part of your case 3. attack his credibility or believability 4. help prove one of your defenses. All of these purposes are to help you win your case and hurt his case.

I like to begin by asking him how many tickets he wrote at that location near the time of this ticket. How many he wrote that day altogether, the day before and the day after. Then ask him details of any of those tickets. If he can't remember the other tickets then how is it that he can remember everything about your ticket. Sometimes the judge doesn't think these questions are relevant. Try to explain they are relevant to the officers credibility and believability. You think he is confusing your ticket with one of the others he wrote. Something is wrong if he can remember everything about your ticket at 11:05 but nothing about the ticket he gave twenty minutes later. If he does remember other tickets then ask if he is mixing up details of your ticket with the others.

Ask if he keeps a log book, reports or anything that keeps track of the number of tickets and locations he gave the tickets. If he says no, then ask how he is evaluated by his superiors as to whether he is doing a good job or not. The judge will understand the innuendo of these questions. The answers are not as important as the questions.

Don't ask questions that will give the officer the opportunity to establish his own credentials and show how qualified he is at doing something like pacing a car or operating a radar gun. Officers are experienced at testifying and are just waiting for questions like "How long have you been a cop" or "How much training have you had with radar guns". They can make a few hours of training sound like they invented the radar gun. It is better to study a particular subject matter and find out what kind of details should be included in the training. You should then ask him specific questions about those factual details of the training.

Next you should ask him facts and details about the scene at the time of the ticket. Ask him if he remembers any other cars, trucks, people, the mailbox on the corner, the big tree on the north east corner or the van parked in front of the bench. If he says he remembers something, then ask him detailed questions about it. If he remembers a vehicle ask the color, make, model, year, anyone in or around it, any markings on the side etc. You can keep him honest by asking about something permanent (like a mailbox) that really isn't there. If he remembers it ask him to point it out on your photo. If there was something that was blocking his view save that question for last so he knows he must tell the truth.

Next go to the detailed facts of how and what happened. Try to show he made a mistake and it couldn't have happened the way he said or he couldn't have seen what he thinks he saw.

Ask him detailed factual questions about how and what exactly happened from beginning to end. Use the detailed notes, diagrams and photos you did for your preparation. Always try to show he was wrong or mistaken. Ask where were you when you first saw me. Where was I when you first saw me. How far away was I from you at that time. How fast was I going at that time. How fast were you going etc. Then check his accuracy with the time and distance chart on page 39. Ask if there was anything obstructing his view at any time. Then show the judge a photo with the sun in the officer's eyes at that time of day or a bush partially blocking his view etc.

Ask many questions about speeds, times and distances. These are hard to answer correctly unless you are really prepared. For example, if he said he paced you for X miles at X MPH then ask how many minutes or seconds that took. Then figure out if he is correct and if he isn't point this out to the judge.

If the Judge asks you any questions that involve speed, time and distances be careful in your answer. If you don't know it's better to say you will have to figure out how many feet per second you were going to answer that question correctly. Then take your time to figure it out or say you don't understand the question. If you can't figure it out it is better to say you don't know than to give a wrong answer.

You must take specifics of your factual situation and turn them into questions unique to your ticket. When you are at the scene say to yourself - I wonder if he would remember this or this and turn those into questions. Write them down as you think of them at the scene. Include questions about how you looked and the clothes you were wearing or anything that is different now versus at the time of the ticket. If you had long brown hair, a beard and glasses but now you have short blond hair and no beard ask him about it. See what he remembers.

The more times you can get the officer to say he doesn't know or remember something, the weaker his case becomes and your case becomes stronger.

INDEX

ORDER FORM

FAX: (714) 666-8663

CALL: (714) 630-3825

MAIL: AVENIR INTERNATIONAL PUBLISHING
1210 N. Jefferson St., STE. G, Anaheim, CA 92807

==

PLEASE PRINT

NAME:_____

ADDRESS:_____

City, State & Zip _____

Your telephone #: _____

==

We accept cash, check or credit card

Credit Card: Visa _____ MC_____

Card No.: _____ **Exp. date**_____

Name on card (print) _____

Sign & date _____

==

Please send _____ @ $15.95 each_____

Shipping & Handling_____$2.00

CA addresses add 7.75% tax _____

TOTAL_____

Quantity discount inquiries are welcome.